TURN
THINK
TELL

Written by Wendy Francis

Illustrated by Joy Weatherall

Connor Court Publishing

The world we live in is very beautiful. Can you think of some other words to describe what you see when you look around you?

There are so many things to see, and there is so much to do and to explore.

TURN
THINK
TELL

TURN
THINK
TELL

TURN
THINK
TELL

TURN
THINK
TELL

TURN
THINK
TELL

This book belongs to:

_____

_____

TURN
THINK
TELL

TURN
THINK
TELL

TURN
THINK
TELL

TURN
THINK
TELL

TURN
THINK
TELL

"Thankyou to Uncle Max Conlon for the use of his Aboriginal Artwork".

Published in 2019 by Connor Court Publishing Pty Ltd
Connor Court Publishing Pty Ltd
PO Box 7257
Redland Bay QLD 4165

sales@connorcourt.com
www.connorcourtpublishing.com.au

ISBN: 9781925826739

Front Cover Design: Maria Giordano
Front Cover Picture: Joy Weatherall
Picture Credits: Joy Weatherall
Printed in Australia

Have you ever walked along a surf beach in Australia and noticed smooth bumps in the sand and wondered what caused them? It is most likely Pipis or surf clams which are small creatures with shells that live just below the sand. They are also known as eugarie (yugari) from the Indigenous Yugarabul language.

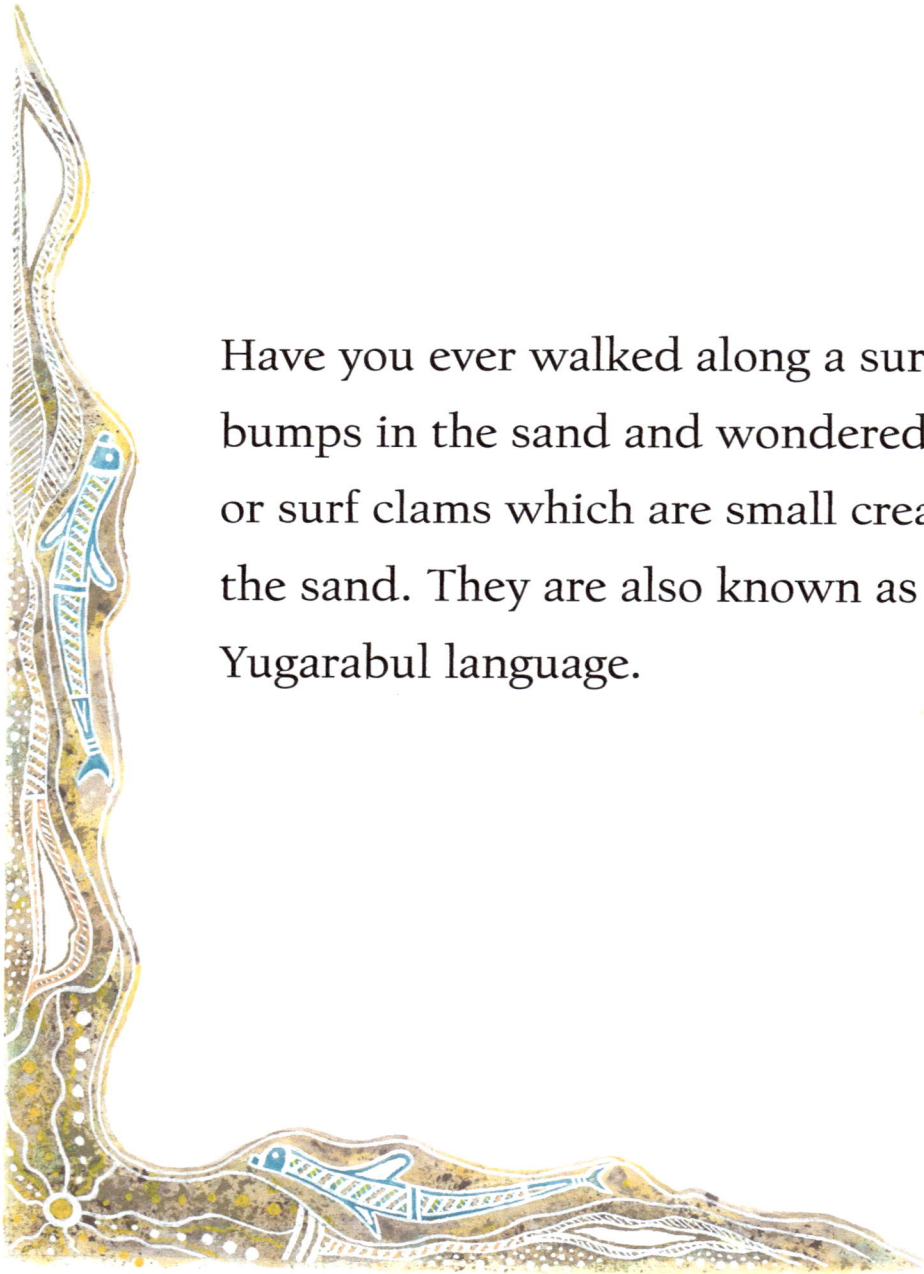

Do you like playing sport? Perhaps you've scored a goal at a soccer match, or maybe you've watched someone hit a 'six' at a cricket game. Whatever sport you enjoy, joining in can be so much fun.

What do you like to do when you travel with your family or friends in a car or a plane to visit a place you've never been before? Do you play games, or do you just enjoy looking out of the window and watching the world go by?

Every day is a new opportunity to experience the world and all that is in it. But before you step out on any adventure, it's important to remember that every explorer needs equipment to prepare for the day and to protect them from danger.

Can you think of some ways that you protect yourself from getting hurt?

Before you walk along the beach, don't forget to put on your sunscreen and hat to protect you from the sun. Otherwise you could get badly burnt.

When you play soccer or cricket, do you use shin pads to protect your legs from accidentally getting hit or kicked? If softball or baseball is your favourite sport, I'm sure you have seen the players wear gloves to protect their hands.

What do you do before you drive off in a car, or fly in a plane? You put your seatbelt on to protect you from harm!

These are all ways that we protect our bodies. But did you know that your mind also needs to be kept safe?

Scientists tell us that our mind and our eyes work together. When you open your eyes, they 'look', but it is your brain that 'sees'. Our eyes work like a camera that sends images to our brain. Sometimes, the pictures we see can make our minds feel uncomfortable, or scared. They might be rude pictures, or pictures of people being mean or even hurting someone. In the same way that we need to remember to use a seatbelt to protect us from being hurt in the car, we also need to learn how to protect our minds from pictures that can harm us.

Do you want to learn how to keep your mind safe? It's very important. Just remember these three words –

TURN

THINK

TELL

Turn your eyes away from rude, unkind or scary images wherever you see them - whether it's on the TV, in movies, on mobile phones or tablets, on billboards, shop advertising, magazine covers or anywhere else.

Think about something good, beautiful or fun straight away - like playing games with your friends, a beautiful flower, a colourful sunset or maybe your favourite animal.

Tell your parent or an adult you trust what you saw and where you saw it.

If someone wants to show you rude pictures on their phone or tablet – what should you do?

Turn your eyes away

Think about something good

Tell your parent or an adult you trust

If you walk into a room and there is a program showing on TV that has pictures that are frightening to see – what should you do?

Turn your eyes away

Think about something good

Tell your parent or an adult you trust

Sometimes when you are driving to school, there are advertising billboards on the side of the road that are not meant for children's eyes. Do you know what to do?

Turn your eyes away

Think about something good

Tell your parent or an adult you trust

When you are walking through the shops, sometimes your eyes might see rude pictures that show someone's private parts. It's important for you to know that every part of our bodies are good, including our private parts. But showing pictures of them is not good, because private parts are meant to be private! If you see one of these rude pictures, what do you think you should do?

Turn

Think

Tell

Our brains are amazing and you are its boss! You can train your brain so that your mind and your heart are protected from harm. Isn't that great? Can you remember the three words that will help you?

Turn

Think

Tell

Whatever is true,

whatever is noble,

whatever is right,

whatever is pure,

whatever is lovely,

whatever is admirable;

if anything is excellent or

praiseworthy,

think on these things.

Philippians 9:8

Note to parents

Reclaiming childhood innocence

The God-given right of children to their innocence is fast becoming a casualty of our post-modern, digital age.

While children are in the care of a loving parent or guardian it is possible, to a large extent, to shield them from violent or sexually explicit material. But outside the relative safety of home they are often confronted with inappropriate imagery and messaging - while travelling, shopping, visiting friends or even at school, on public billboards, shopfront windows, mobile phones, tablets, magazines, music videos or TV.

It is important to be proactive in preparing children before they are exposed to this kind of content. We know that while parents and guardians can teach their children, pray for them and put them on the right path, ultimately a person's character lies in their own choices. Because of this, it is vital that children are taught while they are still young how to make good choices for themselves in terms of what they allow inside their minds.

Children naturally trust their parent or guardian to want what is best for them. A wise adult will use that trust to equip the children in their care with the information they need to make good choices and instill in them a tender conscience that will help save them from a pathway that can lead to a lifetime of grief and regret. My hope is that this book will help you to teach children from a young age what it is to guard their eyes and minds from material that hurts them and that can cause lasting damage in their future lives.

I have suggested three simple choices starting with the letter T to make them easier to remember. Turn, Think, Tell.

But it's not only children who would benefit from these steps!

Wendy Francis

TURN
THINK
TELL

TURN
THINK
TELL

TURN
THINK
TELL

TURN
THINK
TELL

TURN
THINK
TELL

TURN
THINK
TELL

TURN
THINK
TELL

TURN
THINK
TELL

TURN
THINK
TELL

TURN
THINK
TELL

TURN
THINK
TELL

TURN
THINK
TELL

www.ingramcontent.com/pod-product-compliance
Lightning Source LLC
Chambersburg PA
CBHW051027090426

42742CB00004B/103